The Server's Toolbox

A Spiritual and Ritual Guide to Serving the Liturgy

The Server's Toolbox

A Spiritual and Ritual Guide to Serving the Liturgy

George Charle Manassa

© George Manassa 2020

All rights reserved. Except for quotations, no part of this book may be reproduced or transmitted in any form or by any means, electronic or mechanical, including photocopying, recording, uploading to the internet, or by any information storage and retrieval system, without written permission from the publisher.

Published by Parousia Media Pty Ltd
PO Box 59
Galston, New South Wales, 2159
www.parousiamedia.com

Printed in Australia
ISBN: 978-0-6450907-0-3

Quoted versions of Scripture and the Catechism:
Catechism of the Catholic Church Second Edition

The Holy Bible - Revised Standard Version, Ignatius Edition, Copyright 2006 - Second Catholic Edition

Nihil Obstat: Very Rev Wim Hoekstra LSS Imprimatur: + Most Rev Vincent Long Van Nguyen OFMConv DD STL
Date: 13.08.2020

To servers, acolytes, and
discerning seminarians

CONTENTS

Introduction	9
Theology of the Mass	13
Is being an altar server right for me?	19
The benefits of liturgical service	23
Top 10 often forgotten liturgical details	25
Conclusion	33
Recommended reading	35
Ecclesiastical retailers	39
About *The Catholic Toolbox*	41
About *The Rite of Manhood*	43

INTRODUCTION

The liturgy has fascinated many young boys to role play the Mass at home. I too was one of those young boys who would often create vestments from the material of unwanted curtains at home. Then I would cut wafer-style pieces of bread, replay a recorded Mass, and emulate what the priest was saying and doing in the church.

The liturgy is a mystery for many people, because it is simply a series of rituals that result in a supernatural occurrence. I believe that both the structure and beauty of the rituals, with the gestures, along with the spiritual realities in both the prayers and piety, is what draws many people to the mystery and beauty of the Mass.

In my high school years I discerned that I was not called to the priesthood or the diaconate for now. But the call of God came for me to follow him. Not to a Carthusian or Trappist monastery, but rather to serve at his altar, directing the people of God in the pews to prayer and a supernatural dimension. It was in 2011 that I decided I would serve the Extraordinary Form of the Roman Rite, or the Traditional Latin Mass.

Through understanding the depth of rituals and richness in piety, I began to have a renewed perspective on the Ordinary Form of the Roman Rite. In 2012 I began to serve the Mass with greater theological, spiritual and customary understanding, because it was the ancient Roman Rite (from which countless saints have prayed) that gave birth to the new form of Mass today.

I will not discuss in detail the controversies of the Second Vatican Council, however, my simple approach to this dilemma is that what was removed from the Roman Rite in prayer and ritual can easily be restored with a simple understanding of the Extraordinary Form of the Mass. This is why I made the simple decision to learn the form of Mass which came first, before learning to serve the Mass of 1969 of Pope Paul VI. I simply wanted to travel through time, and to have organic growth in my liturgical life as a server. I then proceeded to serve both forms of Mass with a renewed perspective on the Roman Rite, and I continue to fill the areas of ambiguity in gestures, and minor details with that which was carried out in the Extraordinary Form. They are, after all, one rite with two forms.

I continue to serve in my parish today as both a senior server and an acting Master of Ceremonies, and I am gradually growing in my abilities to pray and live the rituals and customs of the Mass for which they were intended.

A key factor to remember is that the spiritual and theological realities are applicable to any Eastern or Western Rite of the Catholic Church. However, the specific ritualistic suggestions of this booklet are only applicable to the Roman Rite. I will discuss in detail the 10 often forgotten customs that I believe should be implemented as much as possible. In no way, shape, or form am I imposing any obligations, and the application of things discussed should always be customised to the particular situation of the liturgical context.

This booklet is designed to help all those who are discerning the priesthood; acolytes; present and discerning servers; and also parents who are seeking to encourage liturgical involvement for their children. As is my custom in providing liturgical instructions, I like to be simple and practical so that you will grow in your appreciation of what I will teach you and be able to practically implement my recommendations.

THEOLOGY OF THE MASS

The Mass, being the re-presentation of the sacrifice on Calvary, the source and summit of our faith from which all the activity of the Church derives and flows, is the centre of our faith. It is vital to understand that the Mass does not exist for our own personal satisfaction, or to cater to our emotional or personal needs. It is there as an act of worship to almighty God. However, the added beauty of the Mass, in all rites and forms in which it exists today, assists us in directing all our senses to the divine work of God in the liturgy. It is the precise sound of chant, incense, bells, and even the architectural beauty of our churches, organically developed over centuries, that clothes the Mass with these external beauties, ensuring our minds and hearts in the true spirit of 'worship' are able to conform ourselves to the unseen spiritual realities taking place.

According to The Constitution on the Sacred Liturgy of Vatican II, paragraph 43:

> At the Last Supper, on the night He was betrayed, our Savior instituted the eucharistic sacrifice of His Body and Blood. This He did in order to perpetuate the sacrifice of the Cross through the ages until He should come again, and so to entrust to His beloved Spouse, the Church, a memorial of His death and resurrection: a sacrament of love, a sign of unity, a bond of charity, a paschal banquet in which Christ is consumed, the mind is filled with grace, and a pledge of future glory is given to us.

His sacrament of love is also within the context of the heavenly worship which we engage at the holy Mass, along with all the angels and saints participating with us and even the souls in purgatory. The Mass has a cosmological nature essentially, and once someone discovers this, coupled with the fact that the bread and wine turn into Christ's Body and Blood, we can't turn back. When we understand this reality, every other aspect of our prayer life will make sense. Deriving from the eucharistic sacrifice is also the Liturgy of the Hours, or Divine Office (that I highly recommend you pray with a breviary or even your smartphone). This form of prayer is second to the holy Mass and is beneficial for our spiritual lives by providing structure to it.

Here are three practical tips in order to live your liturgy authentically in your everyday spiritual life, and to be an example of someone who is a living liturgy themselves:

1. Write down a handful of extracts from the Mass, which can be prayed and applied at work, within the home and during your leisure time. For instance, when I wash my hands, I pray the prayer found in the 'lavabo' (washing of the hands of a priest). The effectiveness of sometimes carrying out a peculiar habit can draw your daily connection back to the source and summit of our faith.

2. Before each Mass, spend 10 to 15 minutes reflecting upon the realities that are about to take place; this can act as a warm-up for your attendance of the worship of God. For about five minutes after Mass it

would also be necessary to reflect on the realities that took place, and to make a thanksgiving. This is basically your chance to digest the spiritual phenomenon that occurred, to assist you in your progress and appreciation of this Sacrament, which we should never take for granted in any place, time or season.

3. The best way to live the Mass is to attend it more often than the Sunday obligation. Though I will not provide you with a precise guideline, it helps to know that each saint understood that they needed the Mass daily to see spiritual progress. Much like how people work out five times per week to see results, start by adding one additional Mass a week apart from Sunday and then increase the frequency every two months, until you can finally achieve daily Mass. The struggle here is that you do not want to become complacent in your attendance, lest it becomes another daily habit or ritual with no living purpose on a personal level. This is absolutely crucial when you are assessing your spiritual growth, which is why the first two tips mentioned

above are so vital in keeping a genuine spirit of participation in this mystery of our faith.

IS BEING AN ALTAR SERVER RIGHT FOR ME?

If you have discerned that becoming a server is definitely the right choice for you, then it is imperative that you understand it is not just simply another logistical way to help the Church. Being a server is radically more than just wanting to 'get involved' and be actively doing something during Mass. It is answering the call to assist the work of Christ through the person of the priest, which we are re-living in the very sequence of events during the sacred liturgy. Being a server should never be about creating a new extracurricular activity to add onto your resume, rather it must be centred on assisting in the dynamic of the sacred actions and rituals, which then bring about the divine mysteries during Mass and other solemn celebrations. It is through the means of the certain prayers, actions and intentions that the Church has standardised and codified formally, that the wafer is able to turn into the Body and Blood of Christ, as with all the other Sacraments.

Here is a short list of questions you must ask yourself before you approach your parish priest, sacristan or whoever has the task of recruitment of liturgical ministries:

1. Has this call to assist Our Lord during the Holy Sacrifice of the Mass and other liturgies come from a genuine desire to serve Him?
2. Has anyone pressured me or constantly urged me to 'get involved' and is this the reason why I am considering it?
3. Apart from having a natural and healthy pride in serving Christ during the liturgy, interiorly, am I greatly disposed to not seek any personal recognition for my work?
4. Am I genuinely someone who is able to direct and not distract the congregation's attention back to prayer, thereby helping them grow in appreciation for the sense of the sacred by my actions and gestures, which bring attention to my faith?

5. Will I be able to die to myself and to my personal habits in order to get myself together to serve the liturgy, so that Christ may increase and I will decrease?
6. Do I have a respect and appreciation for rituals and the importance they have in making divine truths a physical and spiritual reality? Will I be able to respect and carry myself in a reverent way and ensure norms are at play?

These are some very serious and confronting questions that every person who is considering serving must ask himself; or at least, as part of due diligence, the liturgy team or priest within each parish or chaplaincy should ask before recruitment. However, this can sometimes be overlooked because of the current shortage of faithful and prospective servers, and I can be sympathetic in these situations.

However, we must not have a conflict of interest here, since it would be better to have a shortage of servers who are better spiritually disposed, than an abundance who have simply been forced by their parents or who want to keep entertained during Mass. Having said that, I believe that the antidote to some of these issues is simple instruction and education on the part of the parish priest or those liturgically in charge. Sometimes it is from the back door that someone's faith through serving Mass, is then able to be catechised. By simply praying and being close to the altar of God and the Real Presence in the sanctuary, one's faith at any age can grow, and even give rise to a vocation to the priesthood or diaconate.

THE BENEFITS OF LITURGICAL SERVICE

If you are able to purify your intentions along the path of the above questions, you will naturally grow in your liturgical ministry and be able to grow and develop in three very important attributes that will shape your faith holistically:

1. Reverence
By understanding the close proximity to which you deal with the Body and Blood of Our Lord and of the holiness of the sanctuary, you will develop a greater sense of the sacred.

2. Humility
Since liturgical celebrations are not about any individual or person, but only directed

to the worship of God, you will learn what it means to truly die to yourself. By conforming to the foundational and unchanging rituals, you are surrendering yourself to doing God's logistical will.

3. Practicality

You will learn to be a more practical soul in both your personal life and in your spiritual life, especially through your evangelical life in your ordinary circumstances. The reason for this is that the richness in rituals, gestures and the very structure of the worship of God will impress upon your character a sense of greater assertiveness only if taken seriously.

TOP 10 OFTEN FORGOTTEN LITURGICAL DETAILS

1. Dress code
This is something that should never be forgotten when preparing to serve Mass. Shoes should always be of a black, formal nature, and well-kept. To accompany this, black pants and socks should be worn. Hair, as much as possible, should be neatly combed, and extravagant accessories or jewellery that might detract attention from the Mass should be avoided or stored away safely during Mass.

2. Vestments
Based upon your position as a server, the order of priority will inform what needs to be worn, subject to your local customs and

availability. I must first note that it would be a very helpful idea to invest in purchasing your own serving vestments, perhaps with any kind of financial subsidy from your parish or organisation (please refer to the recommended liturgical retailers section at the back of this booklet). There are usually these two options which can be used:

Cassock and surplice - The cassock is black to signify death to yourself, especially during Mass, where your personal life and character are overshadowed by the vestment so that Christ must increase and you must decrease. The surplice is the white garment that covers the top half of your body.

Alb and cincture - The alb is a white liturgical vestment often used in everyday Mass settings. It is white to signify the light of Christ, and the cincture rope that ties around your waist is a reminder of the chains that wrapped around Christ, along with the call to gird yourself in chastity.

3. Hand gestures

The gestures displayed with your hands assist in your personal spiritual disposition and also act as a pointer towards heaven. Take the time to recall the last time you pointed at something in your surroundings. By placing your hands together, you are simply using all of the fingers on your hands to point up to heaven. This should be done during processions and while standing still. Your hands should always be together with your right thumb over your left thumb, at chest height. If you are only using one hand for a task, the other should always be placed on your breast at chest height. When seated it is helpful to have your hands placed flat on your knees.

4. Eyes
The Mass is objectively the worship of God and choosing to serve shows that you have died to yourself and have begun your journey on focusing on prayer and helping others in the congregation do so. Therefore, in this context it translates into being able to communicate with people during Mass on a personal level. Much communication is made through eye contact, hence it is important to avoid eye contact with the congregation during your service. Your eyes should always be either oriented towards heaven or to the liturgical actions taking place. This will assist you in keeping your spiritual and practical focus, and will inevitably help to direct people's attention to prayer when they notice your actions. As a server, you must be a mirror for heaven which then deflects one's gaze from you onto the spiritual realities taking place.

5. Genuflection
Bending your right knee to touch the ground is done before the Blessed Sacrament when

it is not exposed during Mass before taking your seat or when passing by the tabernacle, which is often behind the centre of the altar. This is a sign that we indeed believe in the true presence of Christ. It is absolutely essential to keep this in mind. Often congregations overlook this gesture, and we can only help remind others by demonstrating by example as a server. Indeed, the people are often looking to the servers to provide guidance as to the most appropriate liturgical action or posture.

6. Double genuflection
This gesture is simply genuflecting with both knees on the ground and then bowing. This is done when the Blessed Sacrament is exposed during the elevation at Mass or during Adoration through exposition of the Blessed Sacrament. This demonstrates that there has been a change in the level of exposition of Our Lord, and that it deserves an upgrade of reverence. This also helps the minds of all the faithful comprehend the difference in devotion between the Real Presence in the tabernacle and that of a full exposition. Such gestures both educate and practically train our minds in good habits of reverence for the different formal liturgical prayers and devotions.

7. Bowing
Bowing is a simple gesture, which may be a simple bow of the head or a profound bow from the waist. This is helpfully applied to foster reverence during the moments when the name of Jesus is said within a liturgical context, or when passing by a consecrated altar with no Real Presence in a tabernacle, or prior to consecration. Furthermore, it is helpful to bow to the celebrant (priest or Bishop) when passing them during the liturgy while they are presiding over the Mass, as they are acting 'in persona Christi'. This simply means that they are acting in the person of Christ, and we are therefore venerating Christ, who is at work through the person of the priest.

8. Walking with solemnity
If you have ever observed military parades, the coronation of Monarchs, or the opening ceremonies of parliaments, you will have noticed a certain order to the way in which those involved walk consistently in harmony with one another. Likewise, throughout all liturgical processions - the entrance, the Gospel procession, or the recession at the close of Mass - good posture and straight walking should always be maintained. Furthermore, you should walk with your partner in line with you at all times, as we are the Army of God who is marching to

his altar for the sacrifice, and likewise back out into the world to bring the light of Christ to others.

9. Calmness and subtleness

We have already established that the purpose of the server is to assist the work of the priest in offering sacrifice to almighty God. They are simply there to aid in the work of the divine. We sometimes recognise that we bring the spirit of the world into the liturgy. This can be seen by the way we walk and carry ourselves. We can often be anxious and constantly walk and serve Mass as if we were walking and working in everyday life. In order to become reverent and effective servers, it is important to put ourselves constantly in what could be perceived as 'servers mode'. This would mean that we walk and carry ourselves in a calm and collected manner, just like in military parades and solemn ceremonies outside of the church.

10. Rehearsals and liturgical mistakes

In order to perfect a certain skill it is important to practice in the exact situation which you are preparing for. A soccer team should train in the same context as the very match itself. This is applicable to assigning roles for serving Mass and practising all the obligations and details involved. Small demonstrations and reminders of logistics will help in the harmonious flow of the Mass. It can be very distracting at times during Mass when there are delays and mistakes on the part of the servers, disrupting the order. The objective of each proficient server is to eliminate as many mistakes as possible. What can often define an exemplary server is the ability to keep calm and collected and re-order one's self or the situation if a mistake does indeed happen. Delays or errors are inevitable and will occur whether one has little or great experience. The focus again is not on one's self, but rather on God; so dwelling on mistakes or delays is not helpful. Instead, making a quick note and correcting one's practise is what will help you to grow in your understanding.

The key to remember is that if something does not go as planned, continue in a calm and collected manner, keep reactions to a minimum, and do not amplify more than one should. The main objective is to help things flow smoothly for any liturgical celebration.

CONCLUSION

During the past decade, I have seen the tremendous impacts that occur when the questions which were pondered earlier are asked at the early stages and are able to be satisfied. Furthermore, there are significant positive impacts on the spiritual life of both the servers and congregation when these 10 areas have been improved. What I have noticed is that as a server you can have a tremendous impact on other people's reverence and orientation towards Our Lord when they participate during Mass or any other liturgical celebration. Choosing this ministry with good intentions and taking note of the discussed 10 items will draw you ever more closer to Him, in the spirit of true 'participation' as exhorted by the Second Vatican Council.

RECOMMENDED READING

Archbishop M. Sheehan, *Apologetics and Catholic Doctrine* (The Saint Austin Press, London, revised by Father Peter Joseph, 2010).

Deacon Harold Burke-Sivers, *Behold the Man: A Catholic Vision of Male Spirituality* (Ignatius Press, 2015).

Father John Flader, *A Tour of the Catechism - The Creed* (Connor Court Publishing, 2011).

Father John Flader, *Journey into Truth - Instructions in the Catholic Faith* (Connor Court Publishing, 2014).

Father John Flader, *Question Time 1: 150 Questions and Answers on the Catholic Faith* (Connor Court Publishing, 2008).

Father John Flader, *Question Time 2: 150 Questions and Answers on the Catholic Faith* (Connor Court Publishing, 2012).

Father John Flader, *Question Time 3: 150 Questions and Answers on the Catholic Faith* (Connor Court Publishing, 2016).

Father John Flader, *Question Time 4: 150 Questions and Answers on the Catholic Faith* (Connor Court Publishing, 2018).

Father John Flader, *Question Time 5: 150 Questions and Answers on the Catholic Faith* (Connor Court Publishing, 2020).

Karl Keating, *Catholicism and Fundamentalism* (Ignatius Press, 1988).

Ludwig Ott, *Fundamentals of Catholic Dogma* (The Mercier Press, Ltd., 1958).

Scott Hahn (and Benjamin Wiker), *Answering the New Atheism: Dismantling Dawkins's Case Against God* (Emmaus Road Publishing, 2008).

Scott Hahn, *Rome Sweet Home* (co-written with Kimberley Hahn), (Ignatius Press, 1993).

Scott Hahn, *The Lamb's Supper: The Mass as Heaven on Earth* (Doubleday, 1999).

Stephen K. Ray, *Crossing the Tiber* (Ignatius Press, 1997).

ECCLESIASTICAL RETAILERS

Barbiconi Sartoria Ecclesiastica
Rome, Italy
www.barbiconi.it

Gammarelli
Rome, Italy
www.gammarelli.com

Tradition Ecclesiastical Tailoring
Council Bluffs, USA
www.traditionecclesiasticaltailoring.com

ABOUT THE CATHOLIC TOOLBOX

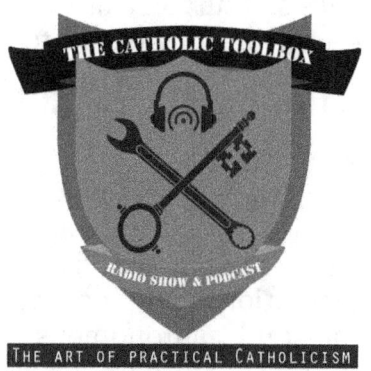

(Radio show, podcast and consultancy)
www.thecatholictoolboxshow.com

The Catholic Toolbox is a radio show and podcast founded by George Manassa and Akita Sanchez, which is broadcast on Voice of Charity Australia (1701AM Sydney) and CRadio online (cradio.org.au). It also delivers public talks on various topics of the faith, customised to the needs of our modern world, equipping listeners with practical solutions to live and directly implement their faith personally in our modern world.

Off-air, it is also a consultancy service, existing to respond to what it calls 'the second dimension of the Church's crisis' — the lack of the practical application of the faith. The Catholic Toolbox consultancy has advised parishes, chaplaincies, apostolates and other Catholic organisations in making direct amendments to the enhancement of their catechesis, liturgical life and pastoral outreach — all in keeping up-to-date with the ongoing changes to the social condition and needs of our modern world.

If your parish, chaplaincy, apostolate or organisation requires assistance in enhancing its performance via a private or public consultation, why not consider an independent and autonomous advisory? We believe that external analysis of the problems facing Catholic organisations in effectively carrying out the work of God can be better addressed using an external advisor. This provides both an objective and detailed diagnosis of obstacles to evangelical underperformance, addressed only thereafter by practical solutions and strategies, to achieve effective outcomes, resulting in the salvation of souls.

ABOUT THE RITE OF MANHOOD

www.theriteofmanhood.com

The Rite of Manhood is a podcast and growing community established by George Manassa and Akita Sanchez to provide men with practical ways to become and grow as men in our modern world. The podcast can be downloaded on all available networks.

On our podcast and community, we also work with women to help men become better fathers, husbands, brothers or sons. The role of women in the development of boys to become virtuous and actual men is vital. This is not about a gender war or any competition for dominance; rather, this is both genders working equally to help each other become who they are for society in all the different levels of relationships that actually demand men to be men.

You can join this project, which is setting out to restore man to his former glory, by assisting to pave the way to create a rite of passage, which can only take place once after the accumulation of skills in all areas of life, and after proficiency and mastery of them; to then finally earn the title of being a man; and then growing in this way of life and becoming the best version of yourself. It is vital that the concept of masculinity is not just discussed in principle, without any practical guidelines, in order to take action immediately.

The three values by which every man must live, and which describe the very nature of what is embedded within the male attributes are to lead, protect and provide. These core values are the litmus test for calling oneself a man, and must be mastered. If we think about it, these three aspects summarise everything you could actually think about within the testosterone-filled creature that prowls the earth, and I will now elaborate on that further:

Lead

To master the fine art of leadership in any aspect of your life, whether it's work, family, the Church or within yourself, it is a prerequisite that you must have carried out what you are leading in. That is to say, you start right at the bottom as a groundsman, not to imply that hierarchy represents leadership in and of itself.

Three practical tips to actually lead and lead well:

1. Strong communication with all parties.
2. Demonstrate what needs to be carried out by example.
3. Let others' light shine and do not desire the credit interiorly.

Protect

This one gets a bit of a bad misrepresentation. Protection comes in many forms within the context of being a man. Physically, we men receive testosterone, which provides them with an objectively stronger physique than females. This is to be used for serving others. The male anatomy itself represents the purpose it exists for, to protect from danger, to fight wars, to work and labour to provide. However, we can be an emotional wreck to others sometimes through our negativity, which is where the symbol of the rose here at The Rite of Manhood comes in, representing the chivalry and gentleness of men. In summary, we protect physically, emotionally, and socially from bad company and from every area of life. We cannot simply cover every practical scenario.

Provide

Providing is probably one of the most controversial topics within our gender-confused society today. However, I would just like to clarify that both men and women should have equal opportunity for working and earning the same income. That is not to say that someone should earn more or be given an unfair advantage, because of gender, because that would in essence disrespect the person and their gender.

So providing, for men, is definitely for the financial aspect, of bringing the bread to the table to feed one's self, one's family and to assist in the community. Men are called to provide spirituality through any form of religion, socially through helping others and one's family network with others, and finally providing input of common sense and skill to social situations — essentially being useful wherever it is needed. That is why we might call someone a handyman. What I am saying is to essentially be a handyman in every aspect of life.

PARTNERS

The Voice of Charity
Australia (1701AM)
www.voc.org.au

Cradio
Cradio.org.au

Parousia Media
www.parousiamedia.com.au

Kreim Media
Kreimmedia.org.au

ABOUT THE AUTHOR

George Manassa is the host and founder of *The Catholic Toolbox* radio show, podcast and consultancy. Co-founded with creative director Akita Sanchez, the program has a large  audience and provides practical strategies for Catholic individuals and organisations to implement their faith personally and to improve evangelical performance around Sydney and NSW. George is also the founder of *The Rite of Manhood* podcast, drawing in men of all faiths united for a common purpose, which is to restore masculinity today.

Inspired by the spirituality of St Josemaria Escriva, George has spent the past decade working in project management to bring God to the secular world in the midst of the ordinary circumstances of daily life. A firm believer in delivering results within the construction and property sector, George is trying to fuse these entrepreneurial and business-oriented mindsets to the Church's approach to implement the New Evangelisation effectively now and for the future.

George has presented and spoken publicly on topics such as liturgy, the development of men, Catholic professionalism, Protestantism, Catholic political influence today, prayer and evangelisation.

www.ingramcontent.com/pod-product-compliance
Lightning Source LLC
Chambersburg PA
CBHW051412290426
44108CB00015B/2260